fOR
me
to
say

for
me
to
say

Rhymes of the Never Was and Always Is

DAVID McCORD

DRAWINGS BY HENRY B. KANE

Little, Brown and Company   *Boston*   *Toronto*

LIBRARY OF CONGRESS CATALOG CARD NO. 76–122534

FIRST EDITION

Grateful acknowledgment is extended to the following for permission to reprint
poems by David McCord which originally appeared in other publications:

"To A Child" is reprinted from *The Crows,* Copyright 1934 by Charles Scribner's
Sons; renewed © 1962 by David McCord.

"How to Draw a Monkey" is reprinted by permission from the January 1969 issue
of *Good Housekeeping* magazine; Copyright © 1969 by the Hearst Corporation.

The poems in the section "Write Me Another Verse" will appear in David
McCord's book *Pen, Paper, and Poem* soon to be published by Holt, Rinehart and
Winston, Inc. The selection is included in this book by permission of the publisher.

"The Tercet," "The Villanelle," "The Ballade," four clerihews, five cinquains, and
six haiku were published in *Horn Book,* August, 1970.

A number of poems in this book were originally printed in the Boston *Globe* in
1970; the poem "Pamela" also first appeared in the Boston *Globe* on October 31,
copyright © 1969 by the Boston *Globe.*

"Mr. Bidery's Spidery Garden" was originally included in Louis Untermeyer's
Fun and Nonsense, a Giant Golden Book, copyright © 1970 by Western Pub-
lishing Company, Inc.

Published simultaneously in Canada
by Little, Brown & Company (Canada) Limited.

PRINTED IN THE UNITED STATES OF AMERICA

Gratefully dedicated
To Helen L. Jones
My stalwart Editor at Little, Brown, 1952-1967

Contents

ix

for
me
to
say

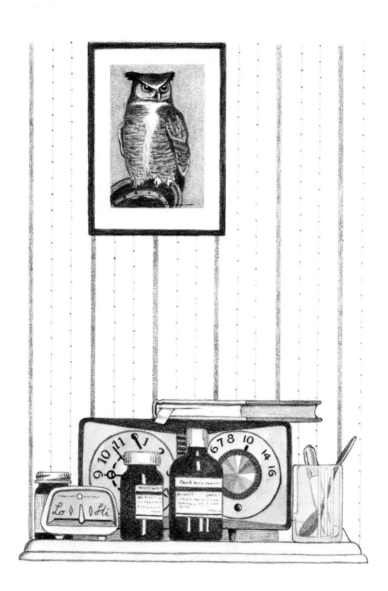

Breakfast

Morning? Morning will produce
a little orange of the juice;
and sure as surely I was born,
a little flaking of the corn,
a little glassing of the white
invention of the cow. Tonight,
though I might ask, might even beg,
to be a-scrambling for the egg,
for bacon sizzly on the fry —
that's not for me, me being I.
Me being I and what I am:
no bit of toast upon the jam,
no chance at creaming of the wheat,
or oating of the meal, to eat.

I meant to say that I'm in bed
and have the bug, the doctor said.

Fast and Slow

The Snail is slow. The swift Gazelle
Could never manage with a shell.

The Snail, without his shell, would squirm
And look a lot like half a worm.

To find him, you would need to peek
Inside some nasty robin's beak.

The poor Gazelle must run to stay
Alive. And that's about the way

It is with Snails and swift Gazelles:
Some have, and some do not have, shells.

4

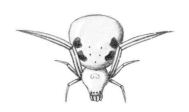

Mr. Bidery's Spidery Garden

Poor old Mr. Bidery.
His garden's awfully spidery:
Bugs use it as a hidery.

In April it was seedery,
By May a mess of weedery;
And oh, the bugs! How greedery.

White flowers out or buddery,
Potatoes made it spuddery;
And when it rained, what muddery!

June days grow long and shaddery;
Bullfrog forgets his taddery;
The spider legs his laddery.

With cabbages so odory,
Snapdragon soon explodery,
At twilight all is toadary.

Young corn still far from foddery,
No sign of goldenrodery,
Yet feeling low and doddery

Is poor old Mr. Bidery,
His garden lush and spidery,
His apples green, not cidery.

Pea-picking *is* so poddery!

Melvin Martin Riley Smith

Melvin Martin Riley Smith
Made do without what we do with.
For instance, did he have a kite?
He didn't, but he had the right
Amount of string to make one fly,
And lots and lots and lots of sky.

Frog Music

In a boggy old bog
by a loggy old log
sat a froggy old frog.

He had spots on his skin;
on his face was a grin
that was wide and was thin.

He was green. He was fat
as an old Cheshire cat.
He was flat where he sat.

While he hoped that a fly
would fly by by-and-by,

it was also his wish
to avoid Mr. Fish,

Mr. Turtle, and tall
Mr. Heron, since all
of them *might* pay a call,

and just *might* be aware
of his grin, skin, and bare

bulgy head and those eyes,
very goggly in size.

So he grinned and just sat,
sat and sat, sat and sat,
looking silly like that.

But no fish saw him grin,
thinking, *Now* he'll jump in!

and no turtle a-cruise
thought him there in the ooze,

as a heron on one
leggy leg would have done.
Not a twitch in him — none.

Isn't life pretty grim
for a frog? Think of him.

But then think of that fly
flying by by-and-by.

LMNTL

"Albert, have you a turtle?"
I'll say to him, and Bert'll
say "Yes! Of *course* I have a turtle."

But if I write,
"Have you a trtl, Albert?"
(as I might)
I wonder if Brtl guess
just what I mean?

We all have seen
a dog's tail wagl,
haven't we?
We all agree
that what a dogldo,
a polywogl too.

We've hrd a brd, grls gigl;
observed how skwrls hnt
for nuts; how big pigs grnt;
know how we feel
on hearing young pigsqweel.

Bbbbs buzz, and ktns play;
bats flitrfly azootowls cry.

Why don't we *spell* that way?
Make ibx look like gnu?
Lfnts too; zbras inizoo?
I do. Do you?

Rain Song

The rain is driving silver nails
into the shingles overhead.
A little girl is playing scales;
she plays them as if something ails
her. Otherwise it's as I said:
The rain is driving silver nails
into the shingles overhead.

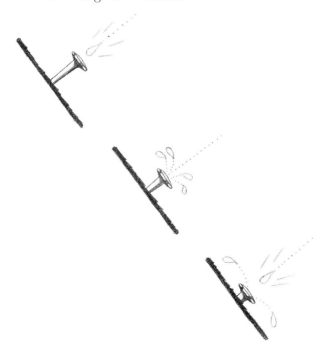

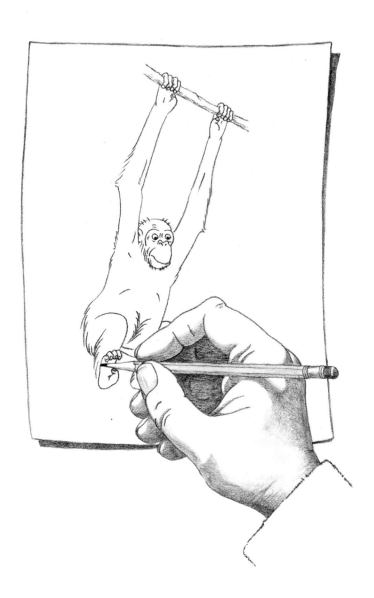

How to Draw a Monkey

To draw a monkey, don't begin
With him, but what he's on or in.
He's in a tree, he's on a limb,
Or was on one. Just follow him
Or follow me — it's all the same,
But easier with me: I'm tame.
You see the branch he's hanging from?
Don't draw it all, though. Just draw some
Of it — about two inches, say.
And draw it so it doesn't sway.
Next twist ten monkey fingers round
It, way up there above the ground,
And hang two arms from them, straight down.
(If you use color, make it brown.
And if the monkey has to scratch,
You'll have to change my method, natch!)
Now join those arms to shoulders, wide
Apart to keep the head inside.
If you can't make a monkey's face,
Look in the mirror! Then you place
The body underneath the head,
But full of life — he isn't dead;
He's just a monkey hanging there
Without his legs. But oh, beware
Of leaving him, forgetting legs!

Remember, chickens come from eggs,
But monkeys, unlike eggs, don't run:
Without two legs it isn't done.
Be sure that to each leg you add
One foot. And if your drawing pad
Is not quite long enough for toes,
Who cares? The monkey, I suppose.

Circus

Caleb likes a good sad clown,
Whose smile is always upside down.
He laughs straight through each foolish show,
With two clowns clowning it below:
One has a gun that he can toot,
One has a horn that he can shoot!
Then Caleb sits and licks the spun
White sugar. Said sad clowns are fun.

Luke (three) prefers the flying rings,
And jugglers who can manage things
And keep them festive in the air.
He also flips before the bear
Who walks flat-foot and shaggy, likes
To balance balls and pedal bikes.
Around his nose he has a strap
(The bear does). Luke has mother's lap.

Theresa, born to ride, is awed
By this big black whose back is broad;
Whose whipless queen in golden gown
Can waltz, cavort, or kneel him down,
Then gallop round in one mad swirl
Of skirt, a frantic act. "The girl —
The queen — leaned back, blew kisses. Gee!
She blew one my way, too," says T.

Louinda

Louinda is a pretty name:
I've never seen or heard it, though.
I think that you can say the same:
Louinda *is* a pretty name.
Please tell Louella what I owe
To Linda. As I say below,
Louinda is a pretty name.
I've never seen or heard it, though.

Little

Little wind, little sun,
Little tree — only one.
Little bird, little wing,
Little song he can sing.
Little need he should stay,
Little *up*-now, away
Little speck, and he's far
Where all little things are.
Little things for me too:
Little sad that he flew.

Sometimes

The clouds are full of new blue sky,
The water's full of sea;
The apples full of deep-dish pie,
And I am full of me.

My money's full of pockets too,
My teeth are full of jaw;
The animals are full of zoo,
The cole is full of slaw.

How full things are of this or that:
The tea so full of spoon;
The wurst so very full of brat,
The shine brimful of moon.

Whistle

I'm talking of a little train whose mother is a Diesel,
And how it skins around a curve as slippery as a
      weasel;
While now and then young Whistle clears his throat
      to give a toot —
You ought to hear him! Mother Diesel thinks he's
      very cute.

One day this little train was flying fast, but on the
      straight:
It carried twenty passengers and lots and lots of
      freight;
And coming to one crossing — reddish lights (left-
      right) a-blink —
Young Whistle, as was usual, thought "I ought to
      blow, I think."

The engineer thought likewise, but what issued was a
      fiz-z-z-z-z.
"There's something wrong with Whistle," said his
      mother. "See what is!"
She said it to the engineer, whose hand was on the
      throttle;
His pipe was in his mouth and full of — well, *you*
      know — of dottle.

He said he hadn't time to look at Whistle: "We're
    behind."
He didn't say behind just what, of course, but never
    mind.
He didn't mind; but Whistle did, and whispered to
    his mother.
(You try to whisper fizzy-fizz: one fizz sounds like
    another.)

His mother gulped a gulp of oil, and in a little gauge
(The engineer had filled his pipe) she let him see
    her rage.
"Now, Mother, take it easy! Don't you think it's just
    a frog
In Whistle's throat? It isn't night; there isn't any fog.

"The sun is bright and chipper. I can see a mile
    ahead."
"Would Whistle whisper to me if there's nothing to
    be said?"
The pipe was lit and drawing well, the window open
    wide;
So engineer reflected: *Was* there something down
    inside

Of Whistle's throat? A gnat? An ant? A June bug
    in July?
If Whistle couldn't whistle . . . "Well, it's nice to
    have him try,"

The engineer was saying — took his pipe out so he
    could.
He'd run a cleaner through it. The tobacco tasted
    good.

There wasn't any cleaner, though, to ram down
    Whistle's throat.
He couldn't use a gargle for the gurgle of one note.
What *was* his note? The engineer confessed he didn't
    know.
His Diesel mother thought it was B flat—the B below

The really truly B, the one above the middle C.
(Just look at your piano — C D E F G A *B*.)
"What difference does it make?" The engineer blew
    bluish smoke.
"I wish" — Ma Diesel rumbled as she said it — "you
    would poke

"Your finger into Whistle. Slow me up or slow me
    down;
You've got to do it anyway, we're coming to a town."
The engineer said, "Mother, gosh! You're living in
    a dream!
Your grampa had a whistle, but he blew himself by
    steam.

"We make a lot of steam on board, but you know
        where it goes:
We heat the coaches with it — ten times everybody's
        toes
Depend on it in winter. We don't make it now.
        Today
It wouldn't work for Whistle — he's electric all the
        way,

"With diaphragm and wires and stuff, just like a
        telephone;
And only sound comes out of him — not steam —
        when he is blown.
That's how it is. Don't *you* forget what makes *you*
        run! It's oil.
We haven't got the steam to bring a bantam's egg
        to boil.

"I tell you what we'll do: at milepost 60 we'll be on
The siding, and the Hanker Chief will thunder by,
        be gone,
Before you say 'Jack Robinson' — who, by the way,
        was Jack?
But just before he does it, coming down the single
        track,

"He'll blow his nose — a friendly blast of greeting.
　　You've got ears,
And obviously you'll hear it. Whistle will. So calm
　　your fears.
I'll pull the cord and close the circuit, ready for the
　　note
That Hanker Chief will thistle into our young
　　Whistle's throat.

"I'll bet you all the air that's in your brakes — I
　　hope you've *some* —
Young Whistle will respond the way drums vibrate,
　　drum to drum."
And sure enough, when Hanker Chief shot by in
　　clouds of dust,
Old Mother Diesel heard the blast — the engineer
　　had thrust

*His fingers in his ears — and Whistle blew as fit to
　　bust!*

Then Mother rolled them back again upon the
　　welded rails.
Young Whistle gave a toot, and since that day he
　　never fails
To blow when he is needed. Mother Diesel has no
　　gripe.
The engineer has trouble, though, with dottle in his
　　pipe.

toot toot

The Wave

As I went up October street,
a windblown wave of leaves to greet
me broke away from someone's lawn.
I thought of sands that I'd been on,
where waves like this came dancing in
to spread their foam out very thin.
These leaves, though, hadn't any foam
or beach on which to roll in home;
they just put up one ragged line
of tumble-turn and intertwine,
all yellow-gold and bronzy-red;
and when the breeze had died or fled,
the wave lay like a jumping rope
with which the children couldn't cope —
all curves and kinks, with none to take
the ends and give it one good shake.

Runover Rhyme

Down by the pool still fishing,
Wishing for fish, I fail;
Praying for birds not present,
Pheasant or grouse or quail.

Up in the woods, his hammer
Stammering, I can't see
The woodpecker, find the cunning
Sunning old owl in tree.

Over the field such raucous
Talk as the crows talk on!
Nothing around me slumbers;
Numbers of birds have gone.

Even the leaves hang listless,
Lasting through days we lose,
Empty of what is wanted,
Haunted by what we choose.

Harvestman

Old Daddy Longlegs, Harvestman,
travels with no particular plan
in mind, so far as I can see:
I meet him wherever he happens to be.
In summer he happens most of all
to be on the sunniest pineboard wall
of a house by a lake. So I say "Hello!
That's a splintery board for stubbing a toe."
He doesn't have toes, of course, but what
do you say to a creature that looks a lot
like a tiny bright pebble with hand-me-down legs,
not a bit good for much except walking on eggs?

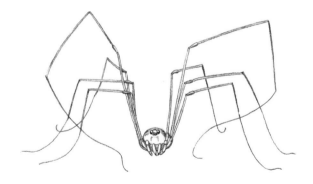

In Winter Sky

Late afternoon: clouds made a hole.
Sun put two fingers through and stole
The golden tops of three or four
Big trees. He would have stolen more;
But clouds, not liking what he did,
Closed up the hole and clapped a lid
On all the trees that they could sight.
Sun whipped his swords out for a fight,
Slashed into them. Each blade he thrust
Shone like a stairwell full of dust
With crosslight on it. Lots of trees
Held up their fiery shields to these.
The clouds, now cut to ribbons, red
With evening blood, closed ranks and fled.

Suddenly

All over the fields there was ice today,
and everybody was out on skates.
It had rained through Christmas, raining away
on the snow, but then in the night the fates,
or whatever it is that decides to freeze,
had dropped the temperature twenty degrees,
and here were the fields like dinner plates
in the shine and flash of the morning sun;
and never, I think, had the kids such fun
as they had on a Christmas day plus one!

Wide fields, big fields, with not any trees:
Skate where you would, and do as you please.
It wasn't just hockey and blow your nose
and lose your mittens and freeze your toes.
It was out and beyond and away on the crust
that was ice you could bend over land you could
        trust.
It was something so wonderful, barely begun,
yet on into moonlight, to over-and-done;
it was skating where no one had skated before,
through field after field till there weren't any more.

It was something just given you — yours by right;
though perhaps you didn't deserve it, quite.

Big Question

Why do you lose things this way?
Why do you say:
I don't choosa lose 'em,
eh?
You lose 'em,
hide 'em
ad infinidem;
whether you read 'em, need 'em,
ride 'em,
or have scarcely tried 'em;
play 'em or break 'em,
people don't make 'em
but you just take 'em,
wind 'em, bounce 'em, renounce 'em,
beat 'em, trounce 'em,
and then can't find 'em!

Bells lose their peals;
You'd lose your meals
And I'd have to repeat 'em
If you didn't eat 'em!

'em 'em 'em 'em 'em 'em 'em 'em 'em 'em 'em 'em 'em

When I Would Travel

When I would travel, I take down
a book like one of yours —
blue binding, is it? yellow? brown? —
itself a book of tours

for which I neither leave the page
nor pause to pack a bag.
I know the language, place, and age:
the country of no flag,

where I am welcome, as are you.
Clouds freckle up the west;
the sun is rising on the view.
Where is it? Who has guessed?

But let me travel far as far
is far, that nameless book,
or one much like it — like a star,
a mountain top, a brook —

is there beside me, so that I
may journey secretly
beyond myself, as by and by
for you it so may be.

Summer Shower

Window window window pane:
Let it let it let it rain
Drop by drop by drop by drop.

Run your rivers from the top
Zigzaggy down, like slow wet forks
Of lightning, so the slippery corks
Of bubbles float and overtake
Each other till three bubbles make
A kind of boat too fat to fit
The river. That's the end of it.

> Straight
> down
> it
> slides
> and
> with
> a
> splash

Is lost against the window sash.

Window window window pane:
Let it let it let it rain.

No Present Like the Time

"No time like the present," they always used to say,
Meaning — *Get Busy! Do You Hear Me? Don't Delay!*
Much better in reverse (it doesn't have to rhyme) :
Simply, simply, *No present like the time.*

Time, you agree, is everybody's gift,
But the packages aren't the same.
The lid of each is there to lift,
Yet only one package bears your name.

Lift the lid a little now each morning,
And what comes whistling out?
A day's supply of time. Almost a-borning
It dies with every breath as you go about

Your work or play. How much of it is in
That package? No one knows. You, least of all.
Time is indifferent to what we begin;
Indifferent also to whether we stand or fall.

Don't waste your time, they say. Waste time you will;
And such as you wish, of course, is yours to squander.
Don't call it wasted when you climb a hill.
Through fields and woods to wander

Is to be young, and time belongs to the young.
It's when you're old that clocks begin to tick.
Play fair with time: his praise so rarely sung.
He is your snail. But oh, his pulse is quick.

The Trouble Was Simply That

the boy wasn't ready for a hat.
The hat, though, was ready for him:
nice crown, good lining, broad brim.
So many people go hatless!
Put your finger down on an atlas —
on land, of course, not on the sea —
and the chances are two to three
the people there go bareheaded.
Some needles just *won't* be threaded;
some heads just refuse to be hatted;
some dogs don't like to be patted;
some shirts don't want to be buttoned;
most sheep dislike to be muttoned.
Few cucumbers crave to be pickled;
fat tummies (ha, ha) are not tickled.

The trouble is just as I said:
Seen a boy with no hat on his head?

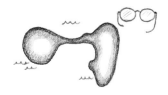

Islands in Boston Harbor

How many islands in the bay?
About a hundred, so they say.
I hope they'll all be there today!

Few people know them. Few can boast
They've been on one and seen the ghost
Of Captain Kidd perhaps — almost.

Down on the map they look so queer:
Unvisited, remote, and drear,
They might be miles away from here.

Down on the map you can't see where
The pirates hid, when they were there.
One island looks just like a pair

Of spectacles; one's like a whale,
And one's a fish without a tail,
And one's a ship without a sail.

Still others seem what they are not:
Napoleon's boot, the moon, and what
Might be a fat smoked ham. A lot

Is in one's island point of view:
The boat I'm on will pass a few.
You look at them. They look at you.

The best have beaches, trees, and rocks,
And cormorants, and gulls in flocks;
But some are faced with granite blocks

Where ancient forts for guns and stuff
Were used by us when times were tough.
Of islands, who can have enough?

Some day a boat will land me right
Upon the shore of one — it might.
And would *I* be a welcome sight!

Just all that island: none but me,
Exploring everything — free, free!
And everywhere the sea, the sea!

Who Hasn't Played Gazintas?

In your arithmetics
the *problem* is what sticks.
The language isn't bound
by spelling, but by sound.
So 3 gazinta 81.
The answer? 27. Done!
In *long* division, I would hint, a
lot of work gazin gazinta.

Or maybe you like Adams — what?
To add 'em up is Adams' lot.
So when you look for something more,
let Adams help you with it. 4
plus half of nine-nine-nine — *precise!*

Well, minusing is also nice.
Take 45, and take it twice
from 93. That's three for me;
And even Mr. Minus, he
can't come much closer, you'll agree.

Then Tums: the sign of which is *x*.
Do 8 tums 1-5-6? It checks
at just one thousand two four eight.
Repeat: 1,248.

Computers work at a faster rate.

Exit x

Let x be this
and y be that,
my teacher says. And I
expecting x to be complex
enough, put wily y
to work. If *vex*
is x^2, *rex*
will equal one-no-three.
But that's not why
x over my
right shoulder laughs at me.

Look: What Am I?

Old friend of man, and made
to slice through root and blade
of grass or weed. The earth was laid
for me to turn.
Up, then down I go,
as sure as I am slow.
What am I?
Spade.

Sow the seed so
the plant will grow.
Up, then down I go,
row after
row after
row after row.
What am I?
Hoe.

In frontier days lean lads
built cabins; dads, granddads
hewed all the beams. Young tads
watched how the strong backs bent.
Up, then down I went.
What am I?
Adze . . . *What?*
Adze.

Out at the woodlot's edge
if you would have the wedge
split clean as privet hedge,
go eat your meat and veg.
Up, then down I go.
To strike it true, my pledge!
What am I?
Sledge.

He who good firewood stacks
knows that my bright head packs
a wallop the hatchet lacks.
Up, then down I go:
I am as nails to tacks.
Watch out below!
What am I?
Ax.

Across the board you draw
one line. The pine smells raw.
Up, then down I go,
just like a jaw
with a juicy chaw
in it. And do I spit!
What am I?
Saw.

Nails are my game: I stammer,
saying things over. Glamor
I never knew.
Up, then down I go.
Who gets me on his thumb
not silent is, but dumb!
What am I?
Hammer.

Eating at the Restaurant
of How Chow Now

Ever eaten Chinese food?
Eaten with chopsticks made of wood,
Holding one chopstick nice and tight?
The other never works just right.

Or if it does, the tight one teeters.
These wooden hinges aren't for eaters
Like you and me. We get a grip
On bamboo shoots, and off they slip!

Thin mushroom slices, peapods, rice,
Hockeypuck meat, need some device
to gather in and underslide them.
Forks are good. But Chinese hide them.

Same with knives: *they can't abide them!*

Under the White Pine

Where the fine pine
by the lone stone

spreads a red bed
for the blown cone,

all the blade shade
fills the green scene.

Keep your cool pool!
Let me lean clean,

with a slack back
to the tall wall

of my own stone,
hear the fall call

of the stray jay
drown the *dee-dee*

chickas say say;
know the slow crow

far away, gay
when his *caw caw*

means but *hey! hey!*
watch a squirrel curl

round a slim limb;
see him creep, leap

through the dim gym
tops of trees . . . Bees,

up the day's haze,
wing in light flight

With a drone tone,
needing night sight

in the live hive.
So it blends, ends

as on dark bark
fails the sun:
                        one

cannot praise days,
heave a high sigh

through the boughs:
                        How's
one to try . . . try?

Story of the Fowse or Fox

(*owse, owsen* is the Scottish variation of *ox, oxen*)

Beyond a whopping owse or ox,
behind his fence a fowse or fox,
investigating rowse or rocks,
has pounced upon a mouse or mox
and flushed a lady grouse or grox,
reminding him of flowse or flocks
of chickens of intowse- intox-
icating scents. The house- or hox-
dog barks just then. That louse or lox
is half and half — half dowse, half dox.
In Reynard's mind, a powse or pox
on *him!* He turns and cowse or cocks
his head. My presence shouse or shocks
him. Exit, then, that fowse or fox,
which leaves me with the owse or ox.

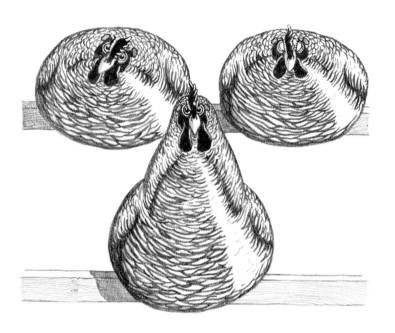

Plymouth Rocks, of Course

I've got three hens. A rooster? No.
He'd dislike laying eggs, and so
I've got three hens. Sometimes they lay;
at first they laid three eggs a day.
It's usually one now; never none.
I don't think hens think eggs are fun.
I feed them corn, wheat, oats, and bran,
and mix hot bran mash in a pan.
I give them grit and oyster shells
and other things the feedstore sells,
including some queer stinko stuff
to make them lay more eggs. It's tough
to be a hen and have to eat
that gravelly grit. And it's no treat
to swallow oyster shells cut fine.
The thought still shivers down my spine!
But hens have crops where shells and grit
grind corn and wheat and oats. And it
seems dandy just to have no teeth
and do your chewing underneath
your throat — all automatic, too;
no mouth to wipe when you are through.
The dirty job, of course, is when
I clean the chicken house. A hen
needs lots of exercise: she'll scratch
the straw back little patch by patch
to find the stuff I've scattered. She
may sing a little song to me
that's nothing like her cackle noise,

but soft and sweet. For who enjoys
life more than happy hens? The cows,
perhaps. They have no crops, but browse
a while and then rechew the hay
as cud which they had tucked away
in stomach number one for storage.
Forget the cows, and let them forage.
I meant to talk about just how
my hens are doing up to now.

More or Less

Add one letter to *widow,*
and that's what you can see through;
but add it after that to *doe,*
by doing so you'll *be* through.
One letter more in *solder*
means lead, not solder, he'll shoot;
and another one added to His *Hon.*
makes something His Hon. can toot.

Now take one letter from *tables,*
and you are ready to tell them;
subtract a different one from *grasses,*
and you can easily smell them.
One letter out of *shout* might mean
that something could well be dead.
If another is dropped from *hate* — well, you
can put what is left on your head!

Strike out what letters from *fancy*
to make yourself feel cooler?
Or what (a lot) from *pinching*
for something found on a ruler?
Delete a little from *tower,*
the result is yours to wiggle;
and, lastly, a smidgen more from *engage*
for some words to make you giggle.

The Look and Sound of Words

You *know* the word *cathedral*.
How about *tetartohedral?*
There's a grass that's called *esparto,*
Which is pretty; but tet-tar-toe,
Plus the *heed-ral* sound just after,
Seems as musical as laughter.

Words often *look* at you. In saying
"Look at *me!*" they see you weighing
All their syllables — the "l's" and
"esses" specially — the bells and
Brightness of their being. So you
Say, "Gee whiz! I *know* you!"

Words have more to them than meaning:
Words like *equidistant, gleaning,*
Paradoxical, and *glisten.*
All you have to do is *listen.*
That's the way words come to settle
In your mind like molten metal.

When they cool, you won't believe you
Aren't old friends. They'll *never* leave you.

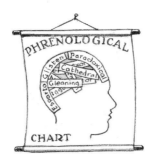

The Game of Doublets

This is a game that Lewis Carroll played,
Called "Doublets." He invented it and made
These rules: Select *two* short words — opposite
In sense, like SNOW and RAIN, or OUT and LIT —
Or else two words which, saying them, we link:
DUCK SOUP; COMB HAIR; perhaps PLAY
          BALL; FURS MINK;
Or two *five*-letter words like BREAD and TOAST.

Now in these few examples *What is most
Important?* Why, that any pairs you choose
Have each *three* letters, *four,* or *five.* Don't use
Six-letter words, or longer, for the trick
Is how to get the *first* word changed as quick —
Excuse me, *quickly* — as you ever can
Into the other: APE (say) into MAN.
How do you change it? Well, you make a chain
Of words that run like this — so have them plain
and full in capitals — LIT BIT BUT OUT.

You see at once just what to do, no doubt.
Remove *one* letter from the *first* word, then
Replace it with another: LIT BIT. When
you do this, put the new one *right smack back*
From where you took the first one. LIT will lack
the L, and so the B goes there and makes
A new word (BIT). You will have made mistakes

If you should jump for WIT or FIT or PIT.
With BIT, though, as the I comes out of it,
In goes the U for BUT; and you see what
The next step is: *remove the B.* You've got
Your O all ready? In? Indeed! OUT! *There!*
I made that up for you, and I can spare
Another: FISH *W*ISH WIS*E* WI*N*E LINE. It's
     wrong
To think they're all that easy, though, for long
Ago (just ninety years) the man who wrote
You *Alice* (which you've read) took off his coat
And went to work on Doublets: APE to MAN!
So simple! APE A*R*E *E*RE ER*R* E*A*R *M*AR MAN.
There's poetry in that — the sound of it:
Ape *are* ere *err* ear *mar* man — *words* that *flit*
Across the page! That is a harder one
Than those we started with, but lots more fun.

This is the place, I guess, where I explain
The *fewer* links you have in every chain,
The better. So, if two of you compete,
The *shorter* chain will win. APE to MAN'S complete
With *five* links in the chain (that's ARE through
     MAR).
Take Mr. Carroll's WET DRY. Here you are:
WET *B*ET BE*Y* *D*EY DRY — *three* links; two are
     tough:
BEY, DEY are generals.* But that's enough

*Look them up in the dictionary.

Of quick short Doublets. No? Well, this EYE LID
Is Carroll's: EYE *D*YE D*I*E DI*D* LID. I bid
You try a new one (mine). Quite hard: SNOW RAIN.
I started wrong: SNOW S*T*OW ST*E*W STE*M* . . .
    In vain
I tried to run it into RAIN from there.

Try it yourself! You'll likely get nowhere.
Then I went back and used a different ploy:
SNOW S*L*OW SL*E*W SLE*D* SL*I*D S*A*ID . . .
    and then, O boy!
I saw the finish . . . *R*AID to RAIN. How fares
The game? You might make up some brand-new pairs
Of words. Or take, from Mr. Carroll's bunch,
PIG (*W*IG W*A*G WA*Y* SA*Y*) STY; or after lunch
WHEAT BREAD, TREE WOOD, GRASS
    GREEN, TEA HOT, MINE COAL,
ONE TWO, PINK BLUE, ELM OAK, GRUB
    MOTH, NICE BOWL.
Or set your sights at changing CAIN to ABEL.
(One hint: begin with C*H*IN.) Or ask Aunt Mabel
If she would like a meaty one with gravy
On *seven* links of sausage: ARMY NAVY.

61

NOTE: PLAY BALL seems to require *nine* links: PLAY pray pram prim grim grin gain pain pail pall BALL. Perhaps you can solve it with fewer. Let me now suggest, as an extension of Mr. Carroll's idea, a Triplet Game, in which one would choose three words, each having some relation to the other pair. Take SKY SUN DAY, which almost solves itself: SKY say pay pan pun SUN pun pan pay DAY. Here is another which looks hard and probably is: COME OVER HERE. *You* try it. I need a rest.

L. CARROLL - Gamester

Ten Nights Before Christmas

"I don't believe in Santa Claus," says Number One.

"I do," says Number Two. "He weighs a ton."

"Couldn't come down *our* chimney, weighing that!"

"You haven't got a chimney one small bat
Could dive down through; but *he* could, though.
There's something magic about the places he can go."

"All that reindeer stuff and a sackful of toys,
And the bunch of Northpole gnomes that he em-
        ploys . . ."

"You hang up your stocking, don't you?" Number One
    says "Yes."
"I thought you did. Full enough in the A.M., I guess?"

"Sure. But that's an inside job. My Dad . . ."

"I know. You woke and saw him?"

                         "Wish I had."

"So you *didn't* see him, eh? Of course not! Yet
You don't believe in a Santa Claus you haven't met."

"I can meet one in any downtown store . . ."

"They're for the birds and bipeds under four!
Look: last year I just *thought* of something I wanted
     a lot.
I didn't *tell* anyone. What do you think I got?
I won't tell *you;* but I *got* it. Now don't think too big."

"Could he get down our chimney with all that rig?"

"See? You don't know enough to say 'No Santa,' do
     you?
Does that do something to you?"

Pease Porridge Poems

1

Mustard when it's hot,
Custard when it's not.

2

Let tapioca share with *you*
These lidless fisheyes in the glue.

3

O summer squash! How posh!
All other squashes taste like galoshes.

4

What is parsley good for?
Gone for good!

It *couldn't* be! It *can't* be!
How I wish it could!

5

Eggplant has a lovely color.
As food, though, how could *anything* be duller?

6

Celery, if you braise it.
Raw celery? *You* praise it.

7

The nearest I come to a cow and her cud
Is when I relax with a fine baked spud.

8

Lens (a Latin word) is what a lentil *looks* like.
A soupy pot of Boston beans is what a lentil *cooks* like.

9

I love a pickle, but detest a cuke.
Please save your stamp and spare me the rebuke.

Just Around the Corner

Just around the corner!
Do you know
that just around the corner's where I go?
I always shiver when I feel
that just around the corner real
things happen, could be happening.
A dozen pigeons on the wing
went by just now. What made them fly?

You need a round-the-corner eye
to answer *that*. But something's up.
A boy is walking with his pup;
or, as I see it, pup has got
a boy upon a leash. They trot.
And round the corner, where he goes,
the puppy's round-the-corner nose
is pulling him. A whistle blew.
But that was round the corner too.
It's where some men in red tin hats
are building up a building that's
all boarded round; but there's a hole
that I can look through like a mole.
They're in a sort of cellar still.
A pump is pumping water till
it gushes from a pipe and flows
along the gutter. Down it goes
to fill the drain (that's just around
the corner) with a gurgly sound.

I hear a siren wailing now.
Some people turn and stare. But how
am I to tell which way the red
fire engine, hook and ladder, sped?
It's just around the corner where
you get to *see* things. Over there
across my street, Apartment Three
looks round the corner. That's not me,
my face glued to the window, though.
I'd be excited and I'd blow
right out the door!
I say once more:

Just around the corner shines the sun;
and just around the corner's where I run.

Make Merry

Make merry, child, make merry:
The day slips by so soon.
Make merry now, this very
Morning. Merry afternoon
will follow, and old Antiquary
Night will bury those unwary
Ere they ever made Make Merry.

Merry child, make merry!
The sound of laughter dies
So quickly, so contrary
Are the wayward cloudy skies.
Down adown adown down derry,
Cheeks as bright and red as cherry:
Merry, merry, make you merry!

Pamela

Pamela — you may call her that —
is making a witch's cloak and hat
for Halloween. She has a broom
up in the closet of her room.

Pamela says each night she tries
to dream of a youngish witch who flies.
The trouble with witches, according to Pam:
"They're all too old; and here I am

just seven. Somehow, I've got the itch.
Why shouldn't I learn to be a witch?
To fly out where it is they fly?
In pictures they are never high

above the ground; yet no one knows
where a witch has come from or where she goes!
I mean to start by the apple tree.
If a witch is there, be sure it's me.

It's mostly kids I'll scare — not you.
I don't know what my broom can do
by way of speed. If dreams work out
the way I think they will, no doubt

I'll get to Tiny Clark's all right.
At least I did the other night.
A practice dream, *that* was. I cleared
the garden wall, and then I steered

right over Tiny's rabbit hutch.
The rabbits didn't like it much.
I saw them — three wild streaks of white —
all every which way in their fright.

Then something woke me." Pam won't say
what woke her. She won't get away
with all this witch stuff, broom or not.
She dreams too much, and talks a lot

of nonsense. Everyone knows *that*.
And with a witch's cloak and hat
and broom on Halloween, you'll see!
But I guess I'll watch that apple tree.

Birds in the Rain

The yellow warblers, the chickadee,
And four of the robins are in that tree,
Under the leaves until the storm
Gives the earth back to the sun to warm.

The rain came hard in a wanted burst,
And pools on the lawn will stop the thirst
Of all our birds. When? When the weather
Clears and they venture out together.

Even the trees are letting through
Some of the sky to where they flew,
Dripping the wings that bore them in,
And bird-breast sodden to the skin.

Between our house and the one deserted,
Lines of a silver blade inserted
Tell me the sun is driving back
The lightning and the cloud attack;

And soon the pleasure of the lawn
Shall be for birds to fare upon,
And the brave robin after worms
Since he has brought the rain to terms.

Hot Line to the Nursery

FATHER SPEAKING. What is that awful noise?

JANET. Hello?

FATHER. I said, *what* is that awful noise?

JANET. Stevie.

FATHER. Stevie, what is that awful noise?

STEVIE. Johnjo.

FATHER. *Johnjo?* Why, he can't . . .

STEVIE. Yes, he can too.

FATHER. Johnjo!

JOHNJO. Goo.

FATHER. Janet!

JANET. Father? Okay. Over.

FATHER. Over my knee, young lady!

JANET. Father, Stevie knows something.

FATHER. What does Stevie know?

JANET. He won't tell me.

FATHER. Well, you tell him I want that *awful* noise
to *stop!*

JANET *(to Stevie)*. He wants that *awful* noise to *stop!*

STEVIE. What awful noise?

JANET. Any awful noise, I guess.

FATHER *(listening)*. No, not *any* noise. Just *that* noise!

JANET. Okay. Do you want to speak to Johnjo again?

FATHER. No.

JANET. Okay. Say okay, Johnjo.

JOHNJO. Goo!

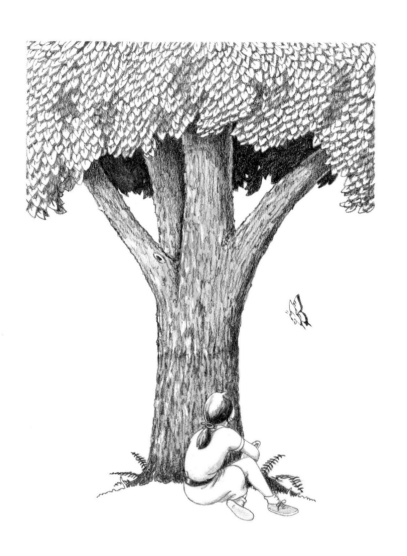

The Tercet
(pronounced *túr-set*)

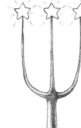

A tercet is a stanza of three lines,
All rhyming; like a pitchfork with three tines.
Or like three stars if none of them outshines

The others. Tercets have a natural grace,
And move along like this in easy pace,
And look up at you face to face to face.

But you can change the rhyme scheme as you wish.
When you go fishing and you bait your hook,
The thing you hope to catch, of course, is fish.

And so with writing tercets. Now I look
For some fresh other rhyme that I can squeeze
In there as with the *hook* and *look* I took

To brighten up this poem. Can a tercet breeze
Into the next this way? Well, so it seems.
Why not? If now we let this third line freeze,

We're back to where we started. On with *dreams!* —
An old poetic word at once redeems
Our one-rhyme scheme. I could go on for reams

Of paper, but I think by now you see
How pleasant tercets are to write. Write me,
Should you have trouble with them. Here I be.

Gone

I've looked behind the shed
And under every bed:
I think he must be dead.

What reason for alarm?
He doesn't know the farm.
I *knew* he'd come to harm!

He was a city one
Who never had begun
To think the city fun.

Now where could he have got?
He doesn't know a lot.
I haven't heard a shot.

That old abandoned well,
I thought. Perhaps he fell?
He didn't. I could tell.

Perhaps he found a scent:
A rabbit. Off he went.
He'll come back home all spent.

Groundhogs, they say, can fight;
And raccoons will at night.
He'd not know one by sight!

I've called and called his name.
I'll never be the same.
I blame myself . . . I blame . . .

All *he* knows is the park;
And now it's growing dark.
A bark? *You hear a bark?*

The Villanelle
(pronounced *villa-knéll*)

I say: Look up this queer word *villanelle*:
A form that has five tercets, one quatrain.
But how which lines repeat, now, who can tell?

I'm sure that you could write one very well;
So never mind what no one will explain.
I say: Look up this queer word *villanelle*.

I think of longer words too hard to spell:
So villanelle should cause you little pain.
But how which lines repeat, now, who can tell?

Just follow me the way you would a bell
And you will need no longer to complain.
I say: Look up this queer word *villanelle*.

Lines one and three in tercet one compel
Attention. Watch for them. Don't ask in vain,
"But how which lines repeat, now, who can tell?"

I leave you with that thought on which to dwell:
Of all these nineteen lines, those two remain.
You can look up this queer word *villanelle;*
And how which lines repeat, now, you can tell.

Turtle

This turtle moved his house across the street.
I met him here about an hour ago.
It is *so* hot, I guess he feels the heat.

Outside, at least, his house looks very neat;
But what goes on inside I do not know.
This turtle moved his house across the street.

No windows, just the four doors for his feet,
Two more for head and tail. Now they don't show.
It *is* so hot, I guess he feels the heat.

He must be tired. I don't know what he'll eat.
Does *he* grow big? Or does his *house* just grow?
This turtle moved his house across the street.

I'll put him near the pond. The grass is sweet.
The dragonflies are fast, but he is slow.
It is so *hot!* I guess he feels the heat.

It's nice to have a house like that, complete
To walk in, float in, sink in mud below.
This turtle moved his house across the street.
It is so hot! I guess he feels the heat.

The Ballade
(pronounced *bal-ódd*)

A ballade rhymes with "odd" and it *is* odd, and not
Like a ballad, which tells us a story that tends
Very often toward death. A ballade has a lot
of surprises, wit, humor; is brief as it blends
This and that. It's a French form, and never offends,
But delights in pure antics. Just eight lines in size
Is each stanza; one rhyme-scheme. By rule each one
      ends
In refrain, like "Beefburgers served only with fries."

A ballade has three stanzas: the prominent spot
Is line eight in each one — the refrain — which
      extends
Your idea, be it silly, or trite, or just rot;
And it's on this eighth line that your topic depends.
Now let's see what our beefburger business com-
      mends.
It appears we can't buy them *alone*. No one tries
To, I guess. I hate fried things! What fool recom-
      mends
A refrain like "Beefburgers sold only with fries"?

I'm that fool. I just *chose* it. I thought I knew what
Would sound pleasant: beefburgers *and* fries are old
      friends.

Most Americans eat them. French fries, when they're
  hot
And quite crisp, aren't too bad; but the vender who
  vends
them — what right has he got to dictate? No one
  spends
extra money for what one dislikes!   If you're wise,
You will *not* write ballades when some rascal defends
A refrain like "Beefburgers sold only with fries."

ENVOY

Did I mention the *envoy* — four lines? One pretends
There's a prince. So begin it now: Prince, I despise
All fried food. *Ugh!* Those nude little spud dividends!
and refrains like "Beefburgers sold only with fries."

Ballade: An Easy One

Of course I find it fun to write
Ballades. Some people don't, alas!
The best ones gallop swift and light
On anapaestic feet.* In class
You'll learn that, like wind over grass,
An anapaest goes ta, ta, *tee;*
Or you can say it: trout, trout, *bass.*
It doesn't matter much to me.

In *this* ballade the line is tight
And short and glitters some, like brass:
Iambic — four feet. Let me bite
It oút / for yoú. / As cleár / as gláss,
We're not deep down in some morass
Of verse; we're sailing smooth and free.
If our next rhyme is *sassafras,*
It doesn't matter much to me.

And yet it *should* because, in spite
Of all your skill, you must amass
A lot of rhyme words — *sprite, might, kite* —
Or you'll be down in some crevasse;

---

*Which is the meter of the preceding ballade.

And you can feel now, as I pass
From *class* to *grass* to *bass,* I see
The end in sight. But I am crass:
It doesn't matter much to me.

Prince, am I finished? Lad or lass,
Ballades may run *you* up a tree.
If my balloon is filled with gas,
It doesn't matter much to me.

The Clerihew
(pronounced *clérry-hue*)

1

The clerihew
Is a tricky form for you.
The first two lines state a fact;
The second two, how you react.

2

Perhaps a name,
Then a line describing the same.
You take off from there.
What you say is your own affair.

3

Samson, you might say,
Had long hair for his day.
What horrid thoughts we harbor
For the first lady barber!

SOREK
Beauty Salon

Miss Delilah
Hair Stylist
Prop.

Specializing
in the latest fad,
CREW CUTS

4

Or think of the planet Mars
All covered with scars,
Canals, and ice caps too;
Not the likes of me and you.

5
Babe Ruth
Is a legend now to youth.
I saw the Babe in action,
Which was a greater satisfaction.

6
The Nottaway
Never got away
To the Platte away
Out thataway.

7
The skunk
Has a lot of spunk.
If the reason isn't plain,
He will gladly explain.

8
Cheyenne
Is sheer magic; but then
So is Broken Bow,
Moosejaw, and Jump-off Joe.

9

You can see the opening line
In these clerihews of mine
Can be long or short. But the zip
In the short *is the crack of a whip.*

10

The dolphin's brain
Is something we would fain
Know a lot more about.
Not so the brain of a trout.

11

When a rooster crows
Everybody knows
The dawn made him do it.
That's all there is to it.

The Cinquain
(pronounced *sing-cáne*)

1

This is
The form of the
Cinquain. The five lines have
2, 4, 6, 8, 2 syllables
As here.

2

Be/gin
That's two/Two more
Now/six/syl/la/bles/and
Then/eight/syl/la/bles/You/count/them
Now/two

3

No/rhymes
All/so/eas/y
Just/keep/count/cor/rect/ly
I'm/di/vid/ing/the/syl/la/bles
For/you

4

Let's build
Something. Guess what?
A cellar first. A floor.
A ceiling. A roof over it.
A house.

5
Four paws,
four feet, head, tail,
two eyes, two ears, a mouth,
a good nose for smelling things. *What?*
A dog.

6
Pen, ink,
table, paper,
an idea, a first line,
more lines, changes, great long pauses,
a poem.

7
Puzzle
chemical too
Get a dictionary
Hexamethylenetetramine*
Got it?

8
Plant seed
Water it well
Sprout divides   just two leaves
Days pass weeks months pass It grows up
Maybe

Héxsa-méthill-een-tétra-mean

9
Two wheels
Handlebars   seat
Two pedals   chain   a brake
Two tires   One of them is flat now
Fix it

10
Behind
Always behind
Following after me
In the way   but still my little
Brother

11
Everything
Small   very small
Neat   orderly   lifelike
Real as the real thing   only small
Doll's House

12
A sound
Far off   haunting
You must listen quite close
Else you won't hear it faintly roar
Sea shell

13
Tough words
Doubling letters
Where you don't expect them
Desiccate and *obbligato*
C B

14
Who sees
The redwoods for
The first time won't forget
Their tallness   ageless look   saying
Always

15
Do you
Care for crickets?
I love their summer sound
Late fall I like one in a house
Chirping

16
What lives
Under water
Very fierce   Eats small fish
Then crawls on land to shed its skin
And fly?

17

Love all
Rivers   They are
Man's friend   ally   power
Near them he builds his cities   Keep
Them clean

18

Try your
Hand at cinquains.
They *show* their form, teach you
To be simple, direct, precise.
Are you?

Haiku
(pronounced *high-coo*)

1
Because it is short,
Japanese three-line haiku
Almost writes itself.

2
Count the syllables!
Five each in lines one and three,
Seven in line two.

3
Syllable writing,
Counting out your seventeen,
Doesn't produce poem.

4
Good haiku need thought:
One simple statement followed
By poet's comment.

5
Take the butterfly:
Nature works to produce him.
Why doesn't he last?

6

Man invents the wheel.
For centuries it runs well.
Today it runs him.

7

Mackerel-shaped cloud
Means a hard rain very soon.
Mackerel will swim.

8

The whistler buoy
Keeps his lips wet in the fog
Quite far from Kansas.

9

Wind, surf, low tide, fat
Horse. Small girl with spurs sails out.
Gulls fly. Her hat flies.

10

All these skyscrapers!
What will man do about them
When they have to go?

11

The bolas spider
Weights a short thread-end with goo,
Twirls it, catching bugs.